# CLIMATE RISK SCREENING SYSTEM FOR MAINSTREAMING ADAPTATION INTO BANGLADESH'S NATIONAL DEVELOPMENT BUDGETING

NOVEMBER 2023

ASIAN DEVELOPMENT BANK

# Contents

# Tables and Figures

# Abbreviations

| | |
|---|---|
| ADB | Asian Development Bank |
| CRS | climate risk screening |
| CRVA | climate risk and vulnerability assessment |
| DPP | development project proforma |
| GED | General Economics Division |
| JICA | Japan International Cooperation Agency |
| MOEFCC | Ministry of Environment, Forest and Climate Change |

# Introduction

Bangladesh is among the countries in the world that are highly vulnerable to climate change impacts. Climate change will affect the country's agriculture, fisheries, ecosystems, environment, ecology, and economy. Addressing the need to mainstream climate change in development activities of Bangladesh emphasizes the need for assessing the vulnerabilities and risks of newly initiated development projects to climate change and natural hazards.

Development partners are already using climate risk assessment tools in their respective projects. The United States Agency for International Development has developed a guidebook for development planners to assess climate vulnerability along coastal areas. The Asian Development Bank (ADB) uses a climate risk management framework (ADB 2014) to assess climate change risks of investment projects and incorporate adaptation measures in project design. The Japan International Cooperation Agency (JICA) uses the JICA Climate Finance Impact Tool for adaptation (JICA 2019a) and for mitigation (JICA 2019b). Since 2014, the World Bank has been using the Climate and Disaster Risk Screening Tools for identifying short- and long-term climate and disaster risks to build resilience in its development projects, policies, and programs. However, such tools are yet to be incorporated into the development planning and budgeting system of Bangladesh. This manual discusses the process of climate risk screening (CRS)/climate risk and vulnerability assessment (CRVA) mainstreamed into the project formulation and implementation system of Bangladesh.

## Climate Change Impacts in Bangladesh

Climate change is a global phenomenon. Scientists project a significant change in global climate systems that will affect countries worldwide, with Bangladesh among the highly affected countries (Ali 1996; World Bank 2000; Sarwar 2005; ADB 2015; United States Agency for International Development 2018; Notre Dame Global Adaptation Initiative 2021). Germanwatch's 2021 Global Climate Risk Index has ranked Bangladesh as the seventh-most affected country in the world based on the annual average of long-term impact data in 2000–2019 (Eckstein, Kunzel, and Schafer 2021). In this 20-year period, the country experienced about 10 climatic disasters annually and an annual average loss estimated at $1.86 billion or about 0.41% of the national gross domestic product (Eckstein, Kunzel, and Schafer 2021). This significant financial loss could be minimized with climate change addressed in the country's development planning and budgeting system. The Bangladesh Delta Plan 2100 estimated that the country will require a total of $38 billion during 2021–2030 for its climate resilience (Government of Bangladesh, Ministry of Planning, Planning Commission, General Economics Division [GED] 2018). On the other hand, the Nationally Determined Contributions of Bangladesh (Government of Bangladesh, Ministry of Environment, Forest and Climate Change [MOEFCC] 2021) estimated a total cost of $176 billion for climate change mitigation actions for the same period.

Bangladesh has long been exposed to various climatological (e.g., drought); hydrometeorological (e.g., cyclone, storm surge, flood); and other geophysical hazards (e.g., landslide and erosion). These major hazards are detailed and mapped in the *Bangladesh Climate and Disaster Risk Atlas (Hazards–Volume I)* (Government of Bangladesh, Ministry of Planning, Planning Commission and ADB 2021). Floods cause the highest damage in the country, followed by cyclones. Asikunnaby et al. (2021) reported that during 2014–2020, floods (including flash floods) impacted 83% of the total affected people and cyclones 17%. Although erosion causes location-specific damage, its damage value can be very high if land value is considered. Drought is also a damaging hazard. Sea-level rise and storm surge cause salinity intrusion along the coastal zone. Flash floods can damage rice production along the *haor* (a bowl-shaped wetland ecosystem in northeastern Bangladesh). Damage because of landslides is limited to the country's east, especially the southeast. Appendix 1 presents the natural hazards affecting Bangladesh and highlights the damages they each cause.

Project development in Bangladesh starts with the formulation of a project idea by relevant agencies with reference to sector plans, five-year plans, or perspective plans. The project idea is developed into a project proposal in the form of a development project proforma (DPP). The DPP passes through a series of screenings and revisions before approval. The sponsoring ministry or division scrutinizes the project for its viability, and selected projects are sent to the Planning Commission for a thorough appraisal. This process is guided by the Ministry of Planning's *Guideline on Approving, Appraisal and Revising Development Projects, June 2022*. The high priority projects (before final approval) get listed as pipeline projects in the Annual Development Plan. An approved project and its allocated budget get included in the plan. However, a project's climate change risks are often considered only superficially while developing the project idea, or at the DPP formulation stage. Hence, this manual intends to provide DPP formulation activities and development planners with guidance for conducting preliminary CRS and detailed CRVA of development projects in Bangladesh.

# Climate Risk Screening and Climate Risk and Vulnerability Assessment

In 2014, ADB developed and has since been applying a climate risk management framework (Figure 1) in all its investments, from the early concept phase through project implementation (ADB 2014). The framework revolves around a two-stage climate risk assessment approach: (i) initial or preliminary CRS at the project concept phase and (ii) CRVA at the project preparation phase. Risk resilience measures incorporated in the project design are monitored in the implementation phase of the project.

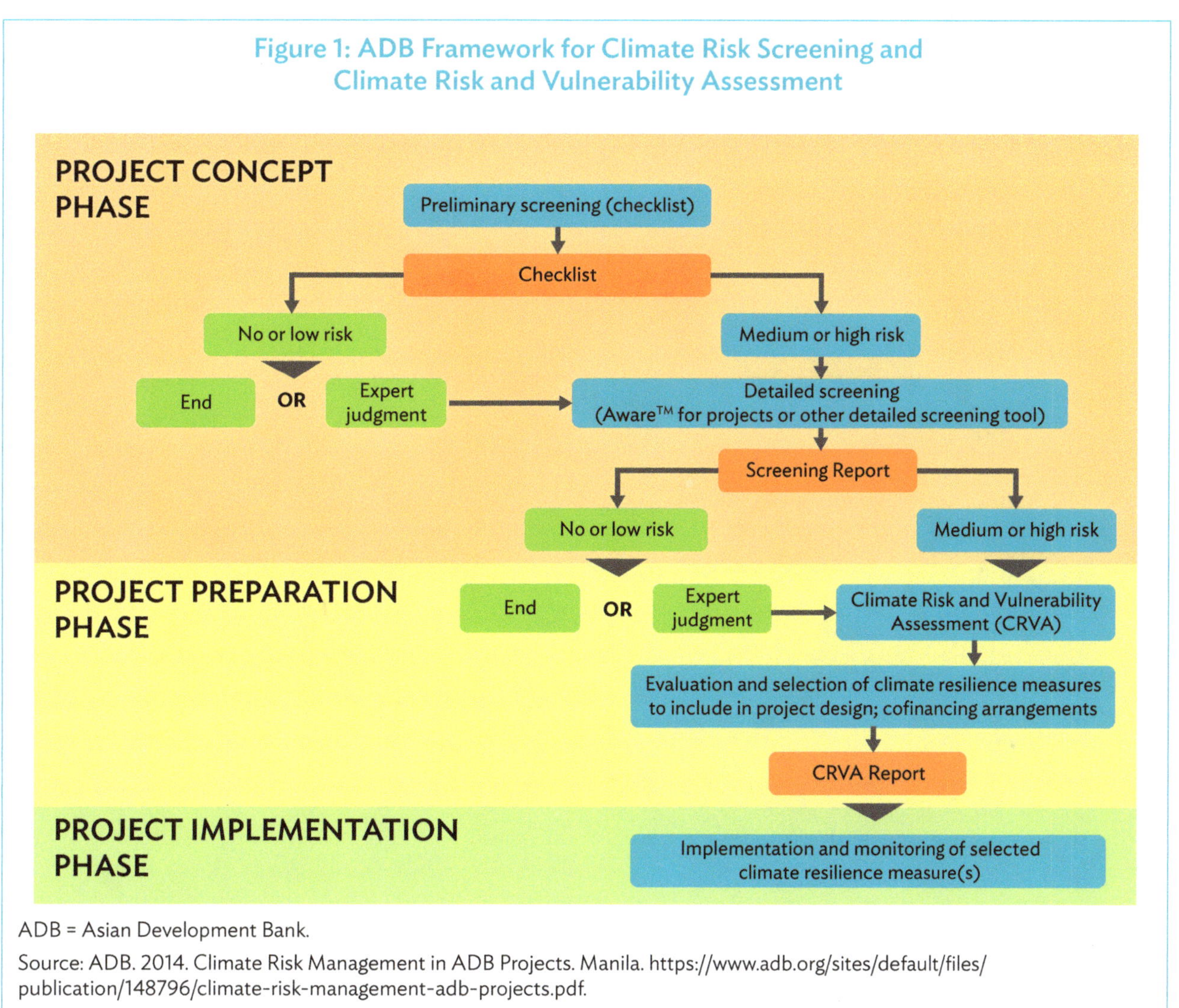

Figure 1: ADB Framework for Climate Risk Screening and Climate Risk and Vulnerability Assessment



ADB = Asian Development Bank.

Source: ADB. 2014. Climate Risk Management in ADB Projects. Manila. https://www.adb.org/sites/default/files/publication/148796/climate-risk-management-adb-projects.pdf.

The idea formulation stage in Bangladesh's development project life cycle is similar to the project concept phase of ADB, except that climate change and disaster risks are not considered in the idea formulation stage in Bangladesh. This manual proposes to have both CRS and CRVA at the project preparation phase in Bangladesh (i.e., at the DPP preparation phase).

A modified CRVA tool based on the climate risk management framework was developed to help assess the climate and disaster risks and vulnerability of public sector development projects in Bangladesh, and to ensure that their designs and subsequent DPPs address significant climate change and disaster risks. In addition, this tool will guide project formulation at the agency, department, or ministry level, as well as project appraisal in the Planning Commission. The steps in conducting the modified CRVA are shown in Figure 2 and discussed in Steps 1 to 9 in the succeeding sections.

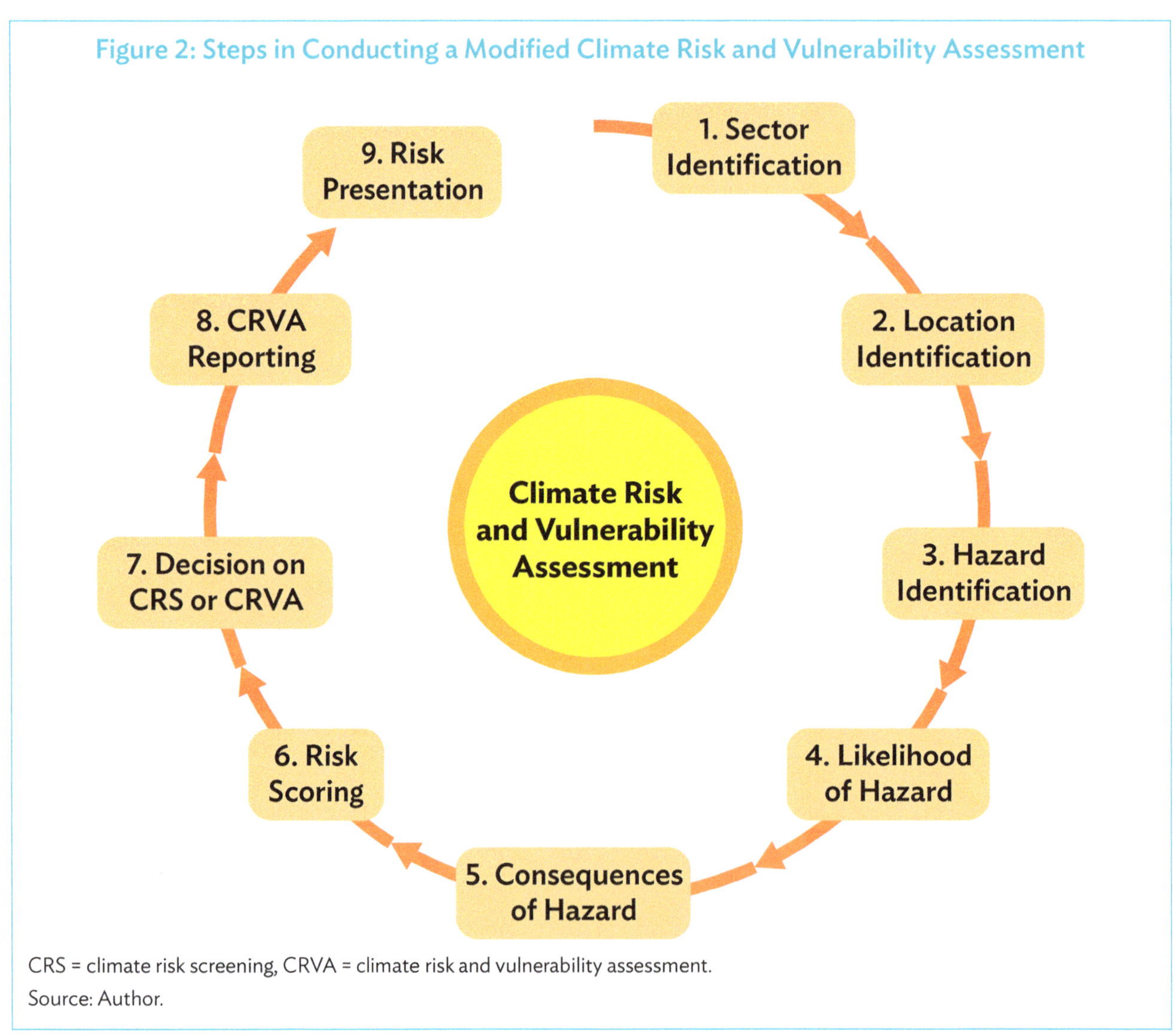



CRS = climate risk screening, CRVA = climate risk and vulnerability assessment.
Source: Author.

# Step 1: Sector Identification

The National Economic Council of Bangladesh approved the country's Eighth Five-Year Plan, July 2020–June 2025 on 29 December 2020.[1] The plan presents 14 sectors under which development projects can be categorized (Government of Bangladesh, Ministry of Planning, Planning Commission, GED 2020), and accordingly the Ministry of Planning reclassified the Annual Development Plan sectors to 16 sectors, which are listed alphabetically below. Sectors of each project must be selected in the first step of CRVA. Please tick (✓) the sector of your project from the following list:

- ☐ Agriculture
- ☐ Defense
- ☐ Digital Bangladesh and information and communication technology
- ☐ Education
- ☐ Environment, climate change, and water
- ☐ General public services
- ☐ Health
- ☐ Housing and community amenities
- ☐ Industrial and economic services
- ☐ Local government, rural development
- ☐ Power and energy
- ☐ Public order and safety
- ☐ Recreation, culture, and religion
- ☐ Science and information technology
- ☐ Social protection
- ☐ Transport and communications

# Step 2: Project Location Selection

Please tick (✓) the district(s) where the project will be located. More than one location may be selected.

| Division | | District |
|---|---|---|
| Barishal | | Barishal |
| | | Barguna |
| | | Bhola |
| | | Jhalokathi |
| | | Patuakhali |
| | | Pirojpur |
| Chattogram | | Bandarban |
| | | Brahmanbaria |
| | | Chandpur |
| | | Chattogram |

---

[1]  Government of Bangladesh, Planning Commission, GED. 2020. *Eighth Five-Year Plan, July 2020–June 2025: Promoting Prosperity and Fostering Inclusiveness.* Dhaka.

| Division | | District |
|---|---|---|
| Chattogram *continued* | | Cox's Bazar |
| | | Feni |
| | | Khagrachari |
| | | Kumilla |
| | | Lakshmipur |
| | | Noakhali |
| | | Rangamati |
| Dhaka | | Dhaka |
| | | Faridpur |
| | | Gazipur |
| | | Gopalganj |
| | | Kishoreganj |
| | | Madaripur |
| | | Manikganj |
| | | Munshiganj |
| | | Narayanganj |
| | | Narsingdi |
| | | Rajbari |
| | | Shariatpur |
| | | Tangail |
| Khulna | | Bagerhat |
| | | Chuadanga |
| | | Jashore |
| | | Jhenaidah |
| | | Khulna |
| | | Kustia |
| | | Magura |
| | | Meherpur |
| | | Narail |
| | | Satkhira |
| Rajshahi | | Bogura |
| | | Dinajpur |
| | | Joypurhat |
| | | Naogaon |
| | | Natore |
| | | Nawabganj |
| | | Pabna |
| | | Rajshahi |
| | | Sirajganj |

| Division | | District |
|---|---|---|
| Rangpur | | Gaibandha |
| | | Kurigram |
| | | Lalmonirhat |
| | | Nilphamari |
| | | Panchagarh |
| | | Rangpur |
| | | Thakurgaon |
| Sylhet | | Habiganj |
| | | Moulvibazar |
| | | Sunamganj |
| | | Sylhet |
| Mymensingh | | Jamalpur |
| | | Mymensingh |
| | | Netrokona |
| | | Sherpur |

# Step 3: Hazards Identification

This CRVA tool considers a total of 10 natural hazards that frequently affect Bangladesh (Appendix 1). Using the table in Appendix 2, this step identifies the hazard(s) for the district(s) where the proposed project will be located. Please tick (✓) the hazard(s) in the district(s) where the project will be located. Select as many hazards as applicable.

☐ Cyclone            ☐ Flood
☐ Drought            ☐ Landslide
☐ Earthquake         ☐ Salinity
☐ Erosion            ☐ Sea-level rise
☐ Flash flood        ☐ Storm surge

# Step 4: Assessing the Likelihood of Hazards

Hazards—Volume I of the *Bangladesh Climate and Disaster Risk Atlas* (Government of Bangladesh, Ministry of Planning, Planning Commission and ADB 2021) presents the likelihood of all hazards in Bangladesh. This step will assess the likelihood of all hazards (Table 1) and classify them into five grades:

☐ Very unlikely      ☐ Likely
☐ Unlikely           ☐ Almost certain
☐ Possibly

The likelihood or level of probability of hazards occurring will depend on the project's geographic location. Based on the likelihood of the hazard in the specified project location(s), as listed in Appendix 3, assign respective scores to each hazard in Table 1, by circling the appropriate number. If the project covers several locations, likelihood will be considered for all locations (by filling out Table 1 for each project location) and the highest rank of likelihood of the hazard will be assigned.

### Table 1: Likelihood of Hazards in the Project Intervention Area

| Location: | | | | | | |
|---|---|---|---|---|---|---|
| | Hazards | Very Unlikely | Unlikely | Possibly | Likely | Almost Certain |
| 1 | Cyclone | 0 | 1 | 2 | 3 | 4 |
| 2 | Drought | 0 | 1 | 2 | 3 | 4 |
| 3 | Earthquake | 0 | 1 | 2 | 3 | 4 |
| 4 | Erosion | 0 | 1 | 2 | 3 | 4 |
| 5 | Flood | 0 | 1 | 2 | 3 | 4 |
| 6 | Flash flood | 0 | 1 | 2 | 3 | 4 |
| 7 | Salinity | 0 | 1 | 2 | 3 | 4 |
| 8 | Sea-level rise | 0 | 1 | 2 | 3 | 4 |
| 9 | Landslide | 0 | 1 | 2 | 3 | 4 |
| 10 | Storm surge | 0 | 1 | 2 | 3 | 4 |

Note: Please identify likelihood for each hazard separately.

Source: ???

# Step 5: Determining the Consequences of Hazards

Exposures, Vulnerabilities, and Risks—Volume II of the *Bangladesh Climate and Disaster Risk Atlas* (Government of Bangladesh, Ministry of Planning, Planning Commission and ADB 2021) presents the exposure and vulnerability index of all districts in Bangladesh. Based on the proposed project's exposure and vulnerability to the hazard, assign respective scores in Table 2 by circling the appropriate box. A bivariate table (template) will be provided to calculate consequences (Table 2).

A series of alternative weights were tried to calculate the consequence (impact) of a hazard. A weight of 0.7 for exposure and a weight of 0.3 for vulnerability were found to generate realistic consequences for Bangladesh, which was also validated by the technical advisory committee. Thus, the formula for calculating consequences can be expressed as

$$\text{Consequences} = (\text{Exposure}*0.7) + (\text{Vulnerability}*0.3)$$

Example: If the exposure of the planned project to a hazard is very high (weight = 5) and vulnerability (likelihood) is high (weight = 4), then consequences of the hazard would be 4.7 = ([5*0.7] + [4*0.3] = 3.5 + 1.2).

## Table 2: Consequences of Hazards

| | | | Vulnerability (0.3) | | | | |
| | | | Very low | Low | Moderate | High | Very high |
| | | Weight | 1 | 2 | 3 | 4 | 5 |
|---|---|---|---|---|---|---|---|
| Exposure (0.7) | Very high | 5 | 3.8 | 4.1 | 4.4 | 4.7 | 5.0 |
| | High | 4 | 3.1 | 3.4 | 3.7 | 4.0 | 4.3 |
| | Moderate | 3 | 2.4 | 2.7 | 3.0 | 3.3 | 3.6 |
| | Low | 2 | 1.7 | 2.0 | 2.3 | 2.6 | 2.9 |
| | Very low | 1 | 1.0 | 1.3 | 1.6 | 1.9 | 2.2 |

| Legend | | Very Low | Low | Moderate | High | Very High |
|---|---|---|---|---|---|---|
| Score of consequence | | 1.0–1.8 | 1.9–2.6 | 2.7–3.4 | 3.5–4.2 | 4.2–5.0 |

| Generalized score of consequence | | 1 | 2 | 3 | 4 | 5 |
|---|---|---|---|---|---|---|

Note: Please calculate consequence for each hazard separately.

Source: ???

# Step 6: Risk Scoring

The bivariate risk matrix method developed by ADB (2017) has been applied to generate a risk score as part of the CRS and/or CRVA of development projects in Bangladesh. This step estimates the risk score by multiplying the scores for likelihood of hazards in the project area as derived from Table 1 and the generalized score of consequences derived in Table 2. Circle the respective risk score in Table 3.

## Table 3: Risk Score

| | | Generalized Score of Consequences | | | | |
| | | Very low (1) | Low (2) | Moderate (3) | High (4) | Very high (5) |
|---|---|---|---|---|---|---|
| Likelihood of Hazard | Almost certain (4) | Moderate (4) | Moderate (8) | High (12) | Extreme (16) | Extreme (20) |
| | Likely (3) | Low (3) | Moderate (6) | High (9) | High (12) | Extreme (15) |
| | Possibly (2) | Low (2) | Moderate (4) | Moderate (6) | High (8) | High (10) |
| | Unlikely (1) | Low (1) | Low (2) | Moderate (3) | Moderate (4) | Moderate (5) |
| | Very Unlikely (0) | Low (0) | Low (0) | Low (0) | Low (0) | Moderate (0) |

| | Risk Level | Risk Score |
|---|---|---|
| Legend | Very Low Risk | 1–4 |
| | Low Risk | 5–8 |
| | Moderate Risk | 9–12 |
| | High Risk | 13–16 |
| | Very High Risk | 17–20 |

Source: ???

> Example: If the likelihood score of a hazard is likely (weight = 3) and the consequences score is high (weight = 4), then the risk score of that hazard is 12. The Table 3 legend indicates that a risk score of 12 corresponds to moderate risk.

It is strongly suggested that risk scores be computed per hazard type pegged to political-ecological units. The total risk score across categories of hazards may be subsequently derived.

## Step 7: Decision on Climate Risk Screening or Climate Risk and Vulnerability Assessment

In effect, the risk score in step 6 will assign risk levels of a project based on project location. A project with a very high risk score (17–20) will be assigned a *very high* risk level and a project with a risk score of 1 will be assigned a *low* risk level. The five risk levels are as follows:

☐ Very low risk  ☐ High risk
☐ Low risk  ☐ Very high risk
☐ Moderate risk

If the risk score is at *very low* to *low* risk (risk score ≤ 8), the project needs to have only a CRS report. **Steps 1 to 6 fall within CRS**. A project with *medium* to *very high* risk (risk score > 8) needs to have a CRVA.

Statement based on risk score (please tick (✓) one)

☐ If risk score ≤ 8, the project may have acceptable levels of climatic risks; a CRS report will suffice.
☐ If risk score > 8, the proposed project has significant climate risks and needs to prepare a CRVA report.

Projects with a risk score ≤ 8 will have a CRS only and will end with the following statement:

*"All hazards (please list the hazards here) have been considered for the proposed project, but no significant impacts have been identified. The findings are outlined in the CRS report."*

This statement will be inserted in the concerned sections of the DPP relating to "climate change and future disaster" (i.e., section 23). Appendix 4 provides the template for the CRS report, which will be appended to the DPP.[2]

---

[2]   The CRS report template is closely patterned after ADB's template for climate change assessment, a supporting document submitted with project proposals for ADB approval.

# Step 8: Climate Risk and Vulnerability Assessment Reporting

Climate risk screening is completed in the conceptual stage of a project. If the risk score is equivalent to *low risk* then it is not necessary to undertake a detailed CRVA for a proposed project. On the other hand, a project with a *moderate* to *high* risk score will require a more in-depth study of climate risks in the form of a CRVA during the project preparation phase.

The CRVA can be done in two parts, as shown in Figure 3: part A—climate risk assessment, and part B—adaptation assessment (see Steps in Climate Risk Assessment and Adaptation Assessment).

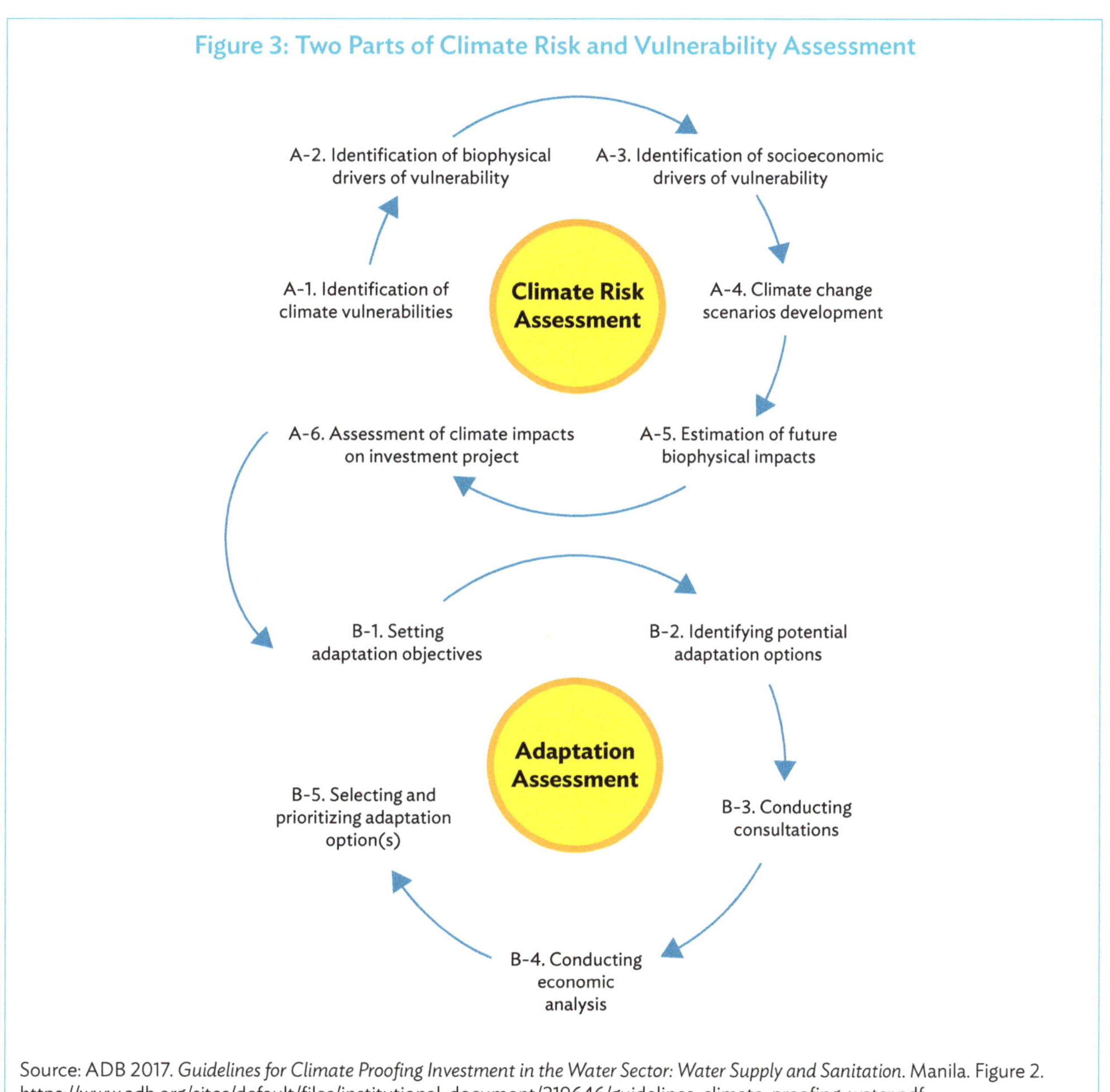

**Figure 3: Two Parts of Climate Risk and Vulnerability Assessment**



Source: ADB 2017. *Guidelines for Climate Proofing Investment in the Water Sector: Water Supply and Sanitation*. Manila. Figure 2. https://www.adb.org/sites/default/files/institutional-document/219646/guidelines-climate-proofing-water.pdf.

Appendix 5 provides a suggested reporting outline for CRVA, and Appendix 6 lists selected potential adaptation options in different ecosystems of Bangladesh.[3] Selection of the most appropriate adaptation options is the final and most important stage of the CRVA report.

## Steps in Climate Risk Assessment and Adaptation Assessment

### A. Climate Risk Assessment

Figure 3 shows the systematic steps in conducting a CRVA. The first part of climate risk assessment will be done via the following six steps:

| | | |
|---|---|---|
| **A-1** | **Identification of climate vulnerabilities** | This step should identify and explain climatic vulnerability in the project area. Climate vulnerabilities can be chosen from those listed in step 3 of the CRVA. |
| **A-2** | **Identification of biophysical drivers of vulnerability** | This step will identify and explain biophysical drivers of vulnerability in the project area. The physical and biological factors that relate to vulnerability include factors such as vegetation and infrastructure. |
| **A-3** | **Identification of socioeconomic drivers of vulnerability** | Socioeconomic drivers such as poverty and income status, livelihood opportunities, and options for alternative livelihood need to be identified here. |
| **A-4** | **Climate change scenarios development** | This step will explain future trends or ranges of climate change in the project area. Decadal scenarios of climatic variables could be developed from secondary sources. |
| **A-5** | **Estimation of future biophysical impacts** | This step will describe future biophysical changes in the project area (e.g., vegetation change, infrastructure projection), as influenced by the climate change scenarios obtained in step A-4. |
| **A-6** | **Assessment of climate impacts on the planned investment project** | This step will explain the overall impacts of climate change on the planned project, as described in steps A-1 to A-5. |

### B. Adaptation Assessment

To adjust to changing climatic conditions, some project components may need to incorporate climate change adaptation solution(s). Appendix 6 lists some adaptation options in different ecosystems of Bangladesh, as identified by the Government of Bangladesh, Ministry of Planning, Planning Commission, GED (2014).

Adaptation assessment will be done in five steps:

---

[3]    The reporting outline was developed under ADB's Action on Climate Change in South Asia regional technical assistance project. The CRVA report will be appended to the DPP when finalizing the project design.

| **B-1** | **Setting adaptation objectives** | This step will define adaptation objectives, such as the need for salinity- or drought-tolerant crop varieties, and the need to protect an area from floodwater of a specific meter height. |
| **B-2** | **Identifying all potential adaptation options** | This step will identify and briefly describe potential adaptation options to achieve the objectives. |
| **B-3** | **Conducting consultations** | The community and other relevant stakeholders should be consulted regarding the planned project, potential climate change impacts on the project, and identified adaptation options. Indigenous knowledge and community preferences could be reflected in this section. |
| **B-4** | **Conducting economic analysis** | An economic analysis should be performed for each adaptation option. (Appendix 6 shows pp. 44–45 of the DPP Manual [Government of Bangladesh, Ministry of Planning, Planning Commission, General Economics Division 2014], which provides details on cost–benefit analysis and economic analysis.) |
| **B-5** | **Selecting and prioritizing adaptation option(s)** | Findings in steps B-3 and B-4 will guide the selection of appropriate adaptation options for the proposed project. Based on community priority and economic analysis, the final adaptation options will be selected. Please select the best adaptation option(s) (up to three) and include them, with estimated costs, in the project component discussions of the DPP. |

# Step 9: Risk Presentation

Estimated climatic risks can be presented in the form of maps. Figure 4 illustrates the combined use of hazard and impact maps to generate risk maps. A combination of historical hazards and current impacts will generate a current risk map. On the other hand, projected hazard maps combined with a modeled socioeconomic impacts map will generate a projected risk map. Risk maps generated using hazard and impact data will be annexed to the CRVA reports.

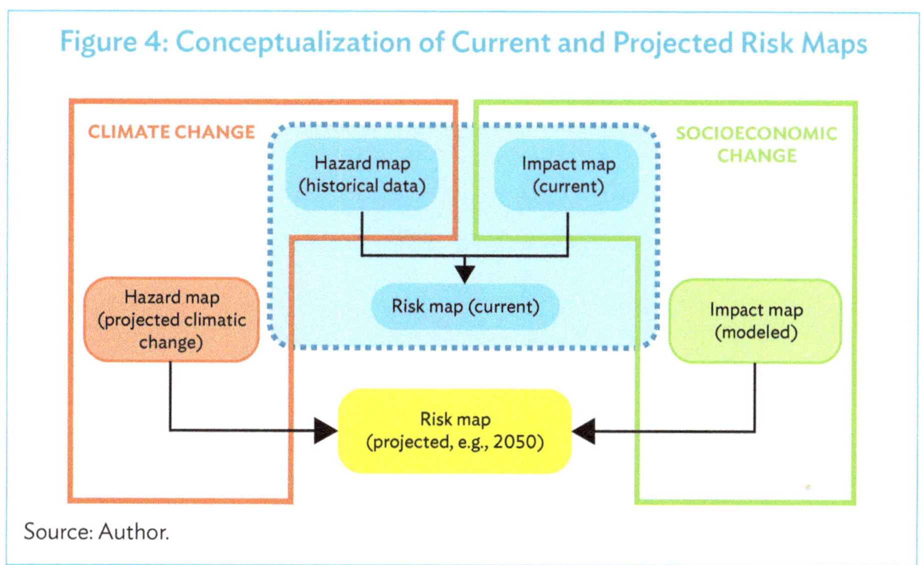

# Conclusion

Climatic and geophysical hazards pose threats to development activities. The Ministry of Environment and Forests (since renamed the Ministry of Environment, Forest and Climate Change) developed the Bangladesh Climate Change Strategy and Action Plan to identify sector focus areas and respective climate action measures (Government of Bangladesh, Ministry of Environment and Forests 2009). Additionally, the government's Standing Orders on Disaster, 2019 help to handle disastrous situations (Government of Bangladesh, Ministry of Disaster Management and Relief 2019). However, a thorough evaluation of the hazard risks will help minimize the climatic and geophysical hazard threats to future investments in development sectors. The CRS and CRVA tools presented in this manual provide a general guideline for evaluating those threats before the project implementation phase.[4]

Natural hazards do not maintain geographic boundaries and their boundaries may vary from administrative ones. This manual generalizes the boundaries of hazards to align them with administrative boundaries. This facilitates government decision-making, as administrative boundary-based decisions are easier to make from a data collection and vulnerability assessment perspective.

Both the CRS and CRVA tools could be downscaled to assess climate change risks of a project at the *upazila* (subdistrict) or union level, for example, through preparing a Bangladesh Climate and Disaster Risk Atlas at the subregional level. The CRS and CRVA tools will help development planners and implementation agencies in Bangladesh in the advance identification of climatic risks of planned new investments. Converting this tool into a digital platform will make it more user-friendly, enabling it to play an important role in addressing climate change in development planning and budgeting system using digital language. The Impact Monitoring and Evaluation Division of the Ministry of Planning may integrate the findings of this tool to monitor the progress of the climate change adaptation component of a project.

The Bangladesh Planning Commission has developed a decision support system, called the Disaster and Climate Risk Information Platform, that considers the CRS and CRVA.[5] An upgraded platform with latest datasets on vulnerabilities and hazards will enhance the application of CRS and CRVA. A series of training programs have been conducted under the National Resilience Programme of the Programming Division, where participants have been trained on CRS and CRVA.

---

[4]    This tool will help determine the risks of climate change and disaster to the project's sustainability and the necessary additional costs, to make project planning more risk informed. For a high-risk area, if the cost of adaptation is very high and cannot be accommodated within the budget ceiling of the sponsoring ministry, the government may not implement it.

[5]    Government of Bangladesh, Planning Commission. Disaster and Climate Risk Information Platform.

For the sustainability of the tools and related databases such as the Disaster and Climate Risk Information Platform, the Planning Division of the Ministry of Planning will expand its existing information and communication technology wing to include additional relevant technical experts, including geographic information system specialists. In 2019, the Programming Division's Public Investment Management Unit was established and became responsible for implementing and monitoring the newly developed reform tools for public investment management of Bangladesh in terms of better project formulation and appraisal. This led to increased cost-effectiveness of projects and ensured that cross-sector issues are well integrated in project-level planning. In this capacity, the Public Investment Management Unit will be responsible for sustaining CRS capacities of development projects.

# Hazards of Bangladesh

Because of its geographical location, Bangladesh is highly prone to climate- and weather-related and geophysical hazards. The Bay of Bengal in the south, mountains in the east, and the Barind track in the northwest have caused natural hazards to persist in Bangladesh for centuries. The funnel-shaped south coast of Bangladesh makes it susceptible to cyclones and storm surges. Bordered by the sea, the country's southern part experiences medium to high levels of soil salinity and  is also expected to face sea-level rise in the near future. The Barind track on the northern and northeastern side of Bangladesh faces frequent drought. Bangladesh is considered to be the largest delta in the world, with the Ganges–Brahmaputra–Meghna river system flowing toward the Bay of Bengal. As a result, a huge portion of Bangladesh's land area experiences frequent floods and flash floods, along with river erosion. In addition, the eastern parts of Bangladesh, comprising the Chattogram and Sylhet divisions, are prone to earthquakes, landslides, and flash floods.

In brief, the hazard profiles of Bangladesh are as follows.

**Sea-level rise and salinity intrusion.** One-third of the population of Bangladesh lives in the coastal region (Ahmad 2019). Of this region, 10% is barely 1 meter above the mean sea level and one-third is under tidal excursion. As such, the 730-kilometer-long coastline is threatened by sea-level rise (Sarwar 2005, 2013). Sea-level rise causes significant salinity intrusion along the coastal zone of Bangladesh, especially in the districts meeting the Bay of Bengal. The salinity problem is severe in the southwestern coastal zone. Soil and water salinity affect agricultural crops, but water salinity affects the country's fisheries resources. About 53% of the coastal region is affected by modest to extreme levels of salinity, which lower the soil fertility of this area (Haque 2006).

A World Bank (2000) study estimated a net reduction of rice production by 0.5 million metric tons by 2050 (from a 2000 baseline scenario) because of salinity intrusion along the coastal zone of Bangladesh induced by a 0.3-meter sea-level rise. This huge loss in rice production was valued at about $247 million. Higher sea-level rise will cause greater loss of rice production. The effects of salinity on agricultural lands and on the production of other agricultural commodities will increase damage manyfold. In addition, sea-level rise will affect the country's human settlements and infrastructure.

**Cyclones and storm surges.** The coastal zone experiences tropical cyclones with wind speeds of different ranges almost every year (Khalil 1992). The deadliest cyclone events happened in 1970 (with a death toll of 500,000), 1985 (more than 11,000 death toll), 1988 (5,708 death toll), 1992 (148,000 death toll), and 2007 (4,234 death toll) (Dasgupta et al. 2011). Tropical Storm Roanu in 2016 caused 27 deaths (Sarwar, Nabi, and Shafin 2016). More recently, Bangladesh experienced two violent cyclones in 2019; six in 2021; and one each in 2020, 2022, and the first half of 2023.[1] The most severe cyclone to make landfall in Bangladesh in 2023 was Mocha, which reached a wind speed of up to 194 kilometers per hour on 14 May 2023 and was 19 kilometers in diameter at

---

[1]    Maximum wind speeds of these violent cyclones ranged from 111 kilometers per hour to about 240 kilometers per hour.

the time, corresponding to a category 3 cyclone. On the open sea, speeds of up to 256 kilometers per hour were measured (category 5) (WorldData.Info 2023).

Tropical cyclones become more devastating and deadlier when accompanied by storm surges. The storm of 1970 resulted in a 9-meter storm surge, which swept away houses, crops, and hundreds of thousands of livestock (Germanwatch 2004).

Cyclones in Bangladesh cause huge economic losses. From 1900 to 2010, cyclone damages were estimated at $4.7 billion–$9.0 billion (Ozaki 2016). The super cyclone of 29 April 1991 caused damage estimated at $1.5 billion (Hussain 2017). Even a weaker tropical storm could cause great financial losses. For example, Tropical Storm Roanu, which hit the Bangladesh coast on 21 May 2016, caused noneconomic loss and damage equivalent to $500 million (Sarwar, Nabi, and Shafin 2016).

**Flood and flash flood.** Because a massive area of Bangladesh is within the estuary of three large rivers—Brahmaputra, Ganges, and Meghna—disastrous floods often hit the country. During the heavy river floods in 1992 and 1998, more than half of the national territory was flooded (Germanwatch 2004). The flood in 2017 affected 3,917,184 people in 24 districts and damaged 309,542 hectares of cropland (ReliefWeb 2017).

Though not so common, Bangladesh also experiences devastating flash floods during the monsoon or pre-monsoon season. Heavy rainfalls and the onrush of water from the upstream Meghalaya hills in India inundate vast areas of croplands in *haors* (bowl-shaped wetland ecosystems) and low-lying areas of northeast Bangladesh. Such floods affect six districts: Habiganj, Kishoreganj, Moulvibazar, Netrokona, Sunamganj, and Sylhet. The flash flood of 2017 caused a loss of $248 million in rice production alone (Abedin and Khatun 2020). Adding the losses in other crops and settlements make it an even bigger figure. The flash flood of May–June 2022 affected nine districts in Sylhet and the *haor* region: Brahmanbaria, Habiganj, Kishoreganj, Moulvibazar, Mymensingh, Netrokona, Sherpur, Sunamganj, and Sylhet (Needs Assessment Working Group 2022). About 94% of Sunamganj district and 84% of Sylhet district were submerged by the flood, affecting about 7 million people and causing damage totaling about $820 million. The flood caused 141 deaths in Bangladesh, including 80 deaths from Sylhet Division alone.

Floods impose a great economic loss for Bangladesh. The floods of 1988 caused asset losses of 5.5% of gross domestic product and the floods of 1998 caused losses of 4.8% (World Bank 2010). The adaptation activities to address increased risks of inland flooding by 2050 in Bangladesh will need $2.7 billion in funding support (World Bank 2010).

**Erosion.** Within the confluence of the three mighty rivers and tributaries, Bangladesh has experienced substantial riverbank erosion. The Ganga, Jamuna, and Padma rivers together have taken away around 150,000 hectares in the last 4 decades (Roy 2014). Erosion in Bangladesh is also because of drought and anthropogenic activities. The coastal zone of Bangladesh faces serious erosion; the highest recorded erosion was up to 120 meters per year along the coast of Bhola District during 1989–2009 (Sarwar and Woodroffe 2013).

Erosion is destroying agricultural land and settlement quietly and permanently. A total of 162,019 hectares of land valued at about $11.78 billion was lost because of erosion along the Jamuna, Meghna, and Padma rivers during 1973–2017 (Hasnat 2018; Anas 2019). Financial losses because of erosion along the banks of smaller rivers and the coastal zone are a few times higher than the losses estimated along the three major rivers.

**Landslides.** Triggered by heavy monsoon rains, southeastern Bangladesh experiences landslides almost every year. For example, during the monsoon season in 2017, rainfall-induced landslides affected 80,000 people in five districts (Bandarban, Chattogram, Cox's Bazar, Khagrachari, and Rangamati). These landslides claimed about 135 lives (ReliefWeb 2017). Heavy rainfall on 12 June 2017 also caused landslides in different parts of Bandarban, Chattogram, and Rangamati districts, damaging properties worth $223 million (Abedin et al. 2020).

**Drought.** Drought-prone areas are mainly located in the northwestern and northern regions of Bangladesh, spread over 5.46 million hectares in the districts of Bogura, Chapai Nawabganj, Dinajpur, Joypurjhat, Naogaon, Natore, Pabna, Rajshahi, and Rangpur. Among the regions, the northwestern Barind tract is especially prone to drought. Droughts are associated with the late arrival or early withdrawal of monsoon rains and intermittent dry spells.

The consecutive droughts of 1978 and 1979 directly affected 42% of cultivated land and reduced rice production by an estimated 2 million tons. The 1997 drought reduced food grain production by about 1 million tons, of which about 0.6 million tons was transplanted aman rice, entailing a loss of about $500 million.

**Earthquake.** Bangladesh has experienced earthquakes and may face major earthquakes in the future because the Barind region is home to the Dauki and Madhupur faults. The Chattogram-Arakan fault is also located in Bangladesh, posing risks as well.

Although Bangladesh is in an earthquake risk zone, only a few studies on the damages caused by the geological hazard are available. Meanwhile, the Asian Development Bank (2015) reported that earthquakes in Bangladesh caused $14 million of damage during 2000–2014. With infrastructure being built and rehabilitated in Bangladesh on a massive scale, even a moderate earthquake could cause huge damage in the country.

# Districts and Respective Hazards

| Division | District | Potential Hazards |
|---|---|---|
| Barishal | Barguna | Cyclone, erosion, flash flood, flood, salinity, sea-level rise, storm surge |
| | Barishal | Cyclone, erosion, flood, storm surge |
| | Bhola | Cyclone, erosion, flood, salinity, sea-level rise, storm surge |
| | Jhalokati | Cyclone, erosion, flood, salinity |
| | Patuakhali | Cyclone, erosion, flood, salinity, storm surge |
| | Pirojpur | Cyclone, erosion, flash flood, salinity, sea-level rise |
| Chattogram | Bandarban | Earthquake, erosion, flash flood, landslide |
| | Brahmanbaria | Erosion, flash flood, flood, salinity, sea-level rise |
| | Chandpur | Erosion, flood |
| | Chattogram | Cyclone, earthquake, flash flood, landslide, sea-level rise |
| | Cox's Bazar | Cyclone, erosion, flash flood, landslide, salinity, sea-level rise |
| | Cumilla | Erosion, flood |
| | Feni | Cyclone, erosion, flood, salinity, sea-level rise |
| | Khagrachhori | Cyclone, earthquake, erosion, flash flood, flood, landslide |
| | Lakshmipur | Cyclone, erosion, flood, salinity, sea-level rise |
| | Noakhali | Cyclone, érosion, flash flood, flood, salinity, sea-level rise |
| | Rangamati | Cyclone, earthquake, flash flood, landslide, salinity, sea-level rise |
| Dhaka | Dhaka | Flood |
| | Faridpur | Erosion, flood |
| | Gazipur | Flood |
| | Gopalganj | Erosion, flood, salinity |
| | Kishoreganj | Erosion, flash flood, flood |
| | Madaripur | Erosion, flood |
| | Manikganj | Earthquake, erosion, flood |
| | Munshiganj | Erosion, flood |
| | Narayonganj | Erosion, flood |
| | Narsingdi | Flood |
| | Rajbari | Erosion, flood |
| | Shariatpur | Erosion, flood |
| | Tangail | Erosion, flood |

| Division | District | Potential Hazards |
|---|---|---|
| Khulna | Bagerhat | Cyclone, earthquake, erosion, flash flood, flood, landslide, salinity, sea-level rise |
| | Chuadanga | Erosion, flood |
| | Jessore | Erosion, flood |
| | Jhenaidah | Flood, salinity |
| | Khulna | Cyclone, erosion, flood, salinity, sea-level rise, storm surge |
| | Kustia | Flood, erosion, salinity |
| | Magura | Drought, erosion, flood, salinity |
| | Meherpur | Drought, erosion, flood, salinity |
| | Narail | Erosion, flood, salinity |
| | Satkhira | Erosion, flood, salinity, sea-level rise |
| Rajshahi | Bogura | Cyclone, drought, erosion, flood |
| | Joypurhat | Drought, erosion, flood |
| | Naogaon | Drought, erosion, flood, salinity |
| | Natore | Drought, flood |
| | Nawabganj | Cyclone, drought, erosion, flood |
| | Pabna | Drought, erosion, flood |
| | Rajshahi | Drought, erosion, flood |
| | Sirajganj | Drought, erosion, flood |
| Rangpur | Dinajpur | Drought, erosion, flood |
| | Gaibandha | Erosion, flood |
| | Kurigram | Cyclone, drought, erosion, flood |
| | Lalmonirhat | Drought, erosion, flood |
| | Nilphamari | Drought, erosion, flood |
| | Panchagarh | Drought, erosion, flood |
| | Rangpur | Drought, earthquake, erosion, flood |
| | Thakurgaon | Drought, erosion, flood |
| Sylhet | Habiganj | Erosion, flash flood, flood |
| | Moulvibazar | Erosion, flash flood, flood |
| | Sunamganj | Erosion, flash flood, flood |
| | Sylhet | Erosion, flash flood, flood |
| Mymensingh | Jamalpur | Erosion, flood |
| | Mymensingh | Earthquake, erosion, flood |
| | Netrokona | Earthquake, erosion, flash flood, flood |
| | Sherpur | Earthquake, erosion, flood |

Source: Author's findings.

# Likelihood of Hazards in 64 Districts of Bangladesh

| Hazard | Very Unlikely | Unlikely | Possibly | Likely | Almost Certain | References |
|---|---|---|---|---|---|---|
| Cyclone | Dinajpur<br>Gaibandha<br>Joypurhat<br>Kurigram<br>Lalmonirhat<br>Naogaon<br>Nawabganj<br>Nilphamari<br>Panchagarh<br>Rajshahi<br>Rangpur<br>Thakurgaon | Bogura<br>Gazipur<br>Hobiganj<br>Jamalpur<br>Keshoreganj<br>Moulvibazar<br>Mymensingh<br>Natore<br>Netrokona<br>Sherpur<br>Sirajganj<br>Sunamganj<br>Sylhet<br>Tangail | Brahmanbara<br>Chuadanga<br>Dhaka<br>Faridpur<br>Jhenaidah<br>Kustia<br>Magura<br>Manikganj<br>Meherpur<br>Munshiganj<br>Narayangan<br>Narsingdi<br>Pabna<br>Rajbari | Bandarban<br>Chandpur<br>Cumilla<br>Gopalganj<br>Jashore<br>Khagrachari<br>Madaripur<br>Narail<br>Rangamati<br>Shariatpur | Bagerhat<br>Barguna<br>Barisal<br>Bhola<br>Chattogram<br>Cox's Bazar<br>Feni<br>Jhalokhati<br>Khulna<br>Lakshmipur<br>Noakhali<br>Patuakhali<br>Pirojpur<br>Satkhira | Islam and Peterson (2009) |
| Drought | Brahmanbaria<br>Chandpur<br>Keshoreganj<br>Kurigram<br>Lalmonirhat<br>Netrokona<br>Noakhali<br>Sunamganj | Bhola<br>Gaibandha<br>Gopalganj<br>Hobiganj<br>Jamalpur<br>Lakshmipur<br>Madaripur<br>Moulvibazar<br>Munshiganj<br>Mymensingh<br>Narayanganj<br>Shariatpur<br>Sherpur<br>Sylhet | Bagerhat<br>Bandarban<br>Barguna<br>Barisal<br>Chattogram<br>Cox's Bazar<br>Cumilla<br>Dhaka<br>Faridpur<br>Feni<br>Gazipur<br>Jhalokathi<br>Khagrachari<br>Kustia<br>Manikganj<br>Narail<br>Nilphamari<br>Panchagarh<br>Patuakhali<br>Pirojpur<br>Rajbari<br>Rangamati<br>Tangail | Chuadanga<br>Jashore<br>Jhenaidah<br>Khulna<br>Magura<br>Meherpur<br>Satkhira<br>Sirajganj<br>Thakurgaon | Bogura<br>Dinajpur<br>Joypurhat<br>Naogaon<br>Natore<br>Nawabganj<br>Pabna<br>Rajshahi<br>Rangpur | Government of Bangladesh, Ministry of Agriculture, Bangladesh Agricultural Research Council (2000) |

| Hazard | Very Unlikely | Unlikely | Possibly | Likely | Almost Certain | References |
|---|---|---|---|---|---|---|
| Earthquake | Bagerhat<br>Barguna<br>Barisal<br>Bhola<br>Chuadanga<br>Gopalganj<br>Jashore<br>Jhalokathi<br>Jhenaidah<br>Khulna<br>Kustia<br>Magura<br>Meherpur<br>Narail<br>Nawabganj<br>Patuakhali<br>Pirojpur<br>Rajshahi<br>Satkhira | Dhaka<br>Dinajpur<br>Faridpur<br>Feni<br>Joypurhat<br>Lakshmipur<br>Madaripur<br>Manikganj<br>Munshiganj<br>Naogaon<br>Narayanganj<br>Natore<br>Nilphamari<br>Noakhali<br>Pabna<br>Panchagarh<br>Rajbari<br>Shariatpur<br>Thakurgaon | Bandarban<br>Bogura<br>Brahmanbara<br>Chandpur<br>Chattogram<br>Cox's Bazar<br>Cumilla<br>Gaibandha<br>Gazipur<br>Khagrachari<br>Kurigram<br>Lalmonirhat<br>Narshingdi<br>Rangamati<br>Rangpur<br>Sirajganj<br>Tangail | Hobiganj<br>Jamalpur<br>Keshoreganj<br>Moulvibazar<br>Mymensingh<br>Netrokona<br>Sherpur<br>Sunamganj<br>Sylhet | Government of Bangladesh, Ministry of Housing and Public Works, Housing and Building Research Institute (2017) created the Bangladesh National Building Code, which divided Bangladesh into four vulnerability categories. No area of the country has been identified as having a "certain" risk of earthquake. | Geological Survey of Bangladesh (2000)<br>Government of Bangladesh, Ministry of Housing and Public Works, Housing and Building Research Institute (2017) |
| Erosion (riverbank and coastal) | Bandarban<br>Chattogram<br>Cox's Bazar<br>Dinajpur<br>Khagrachari<br>Noakhali<br>Panchagarh<br>Rangamati<br>Sunamganj<br>Thakurgaon | Hobiganj<br>Jashore<br>Magura<br>Meherpur<br>Moulvibazar<br>Narail<br>Netrokona<br>Sherpur<br>Sylhet | Bagerhat<br>Gopalganj<br>Joypurhat<br>Khulna<br>Satkhira | Cumilla<br>Dhaka<br>Lakshmipur<br>Madaripur<br>Narayanganj<br>Shariatpur | Barguna<br>Barisal<br>Bhola<br>Bogura<br>Chandpur<br>Faridpur<br>Gaibandha<br>Jhalokathi<br>Kurigram<br>Lalmonirhat<br>Patuakhali<br>Pirojpur<br>Rajbari<br>Sirajganj<br>Tangail | Center for Environmental and Geographic Information Services (undated, as cited in Inman 2009)<br>Sarwar and Woodroffe (2013) |
| Flash flood | Rest of Bangladesh | Not available | Bandarban<br>Khagrachari<br>Rangamati | Feni<br>Hobiganj<br>Moulvibazar<br>Sylhet | Keshoreganj<br>Netrokona<br>Sunamganj | Government of Bangladesh, Ministry of Agriculture, Bangladesh Agricultural Research Council (2000) |

| Hazard | Very Unlikely | Unlikely | Possibly | Likely | Almost Certain | References |
|---|---|---|---|---|---|---|
| Flood | Bagerhat<br>Bandarban<br>Khagrachari<br>Khulna<br>Rangamati<br>Satkhira | Barguna<br>Barisal<br>Chattogram<br>Chuadanga<br>Cox's Bazar<br>Dinajpur<br>Feni<br>Jashore<br>Jhalokathi<br>Jhenaidah<br>Keshoreganj<br>Magura<br>Meherpur<br>Narail<br>Netrokona<br>Nilphamari<br>Noakhali<br>Panchagarh<br>Patuakhali<br>Pirojpur<br>Sherpur<br>Sunamganj | Dhaka<br>Gazipur<br>Gopalganj<br>Lakshmipur<br>Madaripur<br>Mymensingh<br>Narsingdi<br>Thakurgaon | Brahmanbara<br>Cumilla<br>Kustia<br>Natore<br>Rangpur | Bhola<br>Bogura<br>Chandpur<br>Faridpur<br>Gaibandha<br>Jamalpur<br>Kurigram<br>Lalmonirhat<br>Manikganj<br>Munshiganj<br>Narayanganj<br>Nawabganj<br>Pabna<br>Rajbari<br>Rajshahi<br>Shariatpur<br>Sirajganj<br>Tangail | Government of Bangladesh, Ministry of Agriculture, Bangladesh Agricultural Research Council (2000) |
| Landslide | Not available | Not available | Not available | Sylhet | Bandarban<br>Chattogram<br>Cox's Bazar<br>Khagrachari<br>Rangamati | Sarwar (2008) |
| Salinity | North Bengal haor (a bowl-shaped wetland ecosystem in northeastern Bangladesh) area | Rest of Bangladesh | Barishal<br>Magura<br>Shariatpur | Feni<br>Gopalganj<br>Jashore<br>Lakshmipur<br>Narail<br>Noakhali | Bagerhat<br>Barguna<br>Bhola<br>Chattogram<br>Cox's Bazar<br>Jhalokathi<br>Khulna<br>Patuakhali<br>Pirojpur<br>Satkhira | Haque (2006) |
| Sea-level rise | North Bengal | Rest of Bangladesh | Chandpur<br>Chattogram<br>Cox's Bazar<br>Gopalganj<br>Shariatpur | Barguna<br>Barisal<br>Khulna<br>Patuakhali<br>Pirojpur<br>Satkhira | Bhola<br>Feni<br>Noakhali | Sarwar (2005)<br>Sarwar (2013) |

| Hazard | Very Unlikely | Unlikely | Possibly | Likely | Almost Certain | References |
|---|---|---|---|---|---|---|
| Storm surge | Bandarban<br>Bogura<br>Chuadanga<br>Dhaka<br>Dinajpur<br>Gaibandha<br>Gazipur<br>Hobiganj<br>Jamalpur<br>Jhenaidah<br>Joypurhat<br>Keshoreganj<br>Khagrachari<br>Kurigram<br>Kustia<br>Lalmonirhat<br>Magura<br>Manikganj<br>Meherpur<br>Moulvibazar<br>Munshiganj<br>Mymenshingh<br>Naogaon<br>Narayanganj<br>Narsingdi<br>Natore<br>Nawabganj<br>Netrokona<br>Nilphamari<br>Pabna<br>Panchagarh<br>Rajbari<br>Rajshahi<br>Rangamati<br>Rangpur<br>Sherpur<br>Sirajganj<br>Sunamganj<br>Sylhet<br>Tangail<br>Thakurgaon | Brahmanbaria<br>Cumilla | Gopalganj<br>Jashore<br>Madaripur<br>Narail<br>Shariatpur | Barisal<br>Bagerhat<br>Jhalokhati<br>Khulna<br>Pirojpur<br>Satkhira | Barguna<br>Bhola<br>Chandpur<br>Chattogram<br>Cox's Bazar<br>Feni<br>Lakshmipur<br>Noakhali<br>Patuakhali | Sarwar (2013) |

Source: Author.

# Climate Risk Screening Reporting Template

## I. Basic Project Information

| |
|---|
| **Project Title:** |
| **Project Cost** (million Tk): |
| **Location:** |
| **Sector:** |
| **Objectives:** |
| **Brief Description** *(particularly highlighting aspects of the project that could be affected by weather or climate conditions and natural hazards, maximum of 1,000 words):* |

## II. Summary of Climate Risk Screening and Assessment

| **A. Sensitivity of Project Component(s) to Climate or Weather Conditions and Sea Level** | |
|---|---|
| *Describe how climate or weather conditions (e.g., temperature and seasonal contrast, rainfall amount and seasonality, wind, solar radiation) and sea level could affect the relevant project component(s).* | |
| *Examples*<br>Project component<br>1.   *Construction of a road pavement*<br>2.   *Construction of a new river-crossing bridge*<br>3. | *Examples*<br>Sensitivity to climate or weather conditions and sea level<br>1.   *Winter and summer temperature contrast*<br>2.   *Intensity and frequency of heavy rainfall events*<br>3. |

<table>
<tr><td colspan="2">B.    Climate Risk Screening</td></tr>
<tr>
<td>Risk topic<br>[Examples]<br>Temperature increase<br>Rainfall increase</td>
<td>Description of the risk<br>[Examples]<br>Bridge freeboard allowance calculated with current climate statistics may be insufficient with projected increase in rainfall intensity</td>
</tr>
<tr><td colspan="2">

**C.    Climate Risk and Adaptation Assessment**

*If the climate risk screening ranks the project as medium or high risk, a more in-depth climate risk and vulnerability assessment (CRVA) shall be carried out to identify the nature and magnitude of climate risks to the different components of the project, and to identify and assess potential adaptation options for managing the risks.*

*Summarize the key findings from the CRVA, including the following:*
1.    Overall methodology for the risk and adaptation assessment, data and key assumptions used
2.    Key climate risks to the relevant components of the project
3.    Adaptation options identified and prioritized for managing the risks

</td></tr>
<tr><td colspan="2">

**D.    Climate Risk Screening Tool or Procedure Used** (specify):
*(For example, CRVA Tool for Screening Climate Change Risks of Development Project)*

</td></tr>
</table>

**III.  Climate Adaptation Plans Within the Project** *(if applicable)*
*Based on the adaptation options identified in the climate risk assessment discussed in section II, list all activities being included in the project to address identified climate risks; for each adaptation activity, provide an estimate of adaptation finance and the justification for the estimate.*

| Adaptation Activity | Target Climate Risk | Estimated Adaptation Finance (million Tk) | Adaptation Finance Justification |
|---|---|---|---|
|  |  |  |  |
|  |  |  |  |
|  |  |  |  |
|  |  |  |  |
|  |  |  |  |
|  |  |  |  |
|  |  |  |  |

## IV.  Climate Mitigation Plans Within the Project *(if applicable)*

*Describe project activities, indicators, and associated finance aimed at reducing greenhouse gas emissions and budgetary allocations; for each mitigation activity, provide an estimate of associated cost and the justification for the estimate.*

| Mitigation Activity | Estimated Greenhouse Gas Emissions Reduction (tons of carbon dioxide equivalent/year) | Estimated Mitigation Finance (million Tk) | Mitigation Finance Justification |
|---|---|---|---|
|  |  |  |  |
|  |  |  |  |
|  |  |  |  |
|  |  |  |  |
|  |  |  |  |
|  |  |  |  |
|  |  |  |  |

Source: Modified Asian Development Bank climate change assessment template.

# Climate Risk and Vulnerability Assessment Reporting Outline

| | |
|---|---|
| **Project Title:** | |
| **Project Cost** (million Tk): | |
| **Location:** | |
| **Sector:** | |
| **Objectives:** | |
| **Brief Description** (*particularly highlighting aspects of the project that could be affected by weather or climate conditions and natural hazards, maximum of 1,000 words*): | |

**Executive Summary**

1. **INTRODUCTION**
   *Includes a situational background of the project sector in the country, in general. The following are suggested topics:*
   Background
   Concept of risk and vulnerability
   Sector climate risk and vulnerability (may include definition of terms)
   Sector's regulatory, legal, institutional, and policy frameworks in the country
   Report structure

2. **PROJECT DESCRIPTION**
   *Includes specific information about the project sector or subsectors being assessed:*
   Project profile
   Objective(s) of the climate risk and vulnerability assessment or rationale
   Methodology, scope, and limitations
   Data inventory and collection (includes current and future climate)
   Summary

3.  **CLIMATE CHANGE HAZARDS ON THE PROJECT SECTOR AND SUBSECTORS**
    *Include only the relevant factors. The following are suggested:*
    A.  Baseline assessment
        - Cyclones and storm surges—observed trends
        - Flood or flash flood hazard susceptibility
        - Soil erosion
        - Climate: rainfall, temperature, extreme events, observed trends
        - Drought hazard susceptibility
        - Sea-level rise and salinity intrusion
        - Geophysical: earthquake hazards
        - Topography
    B.  Assessments using future projections (select the appropriate timelines suited to the sector being analyzed, such as 2025, 2050, and 2100)
        - Rainfall change
        - Temperature
        - Extreme events
        - Sea-level change (possible that sea level is not changing or is even decreasing)
        - Cyclones and storm surge

4.  **CLIMATE RISK AND VULNERABILITY ASSESSMENT**
    *There are many ways to carry this out such as through impact modeling, geographic information system layering, or descriptive impact matrix.*
        - Hazard and exposure characterization: defines what hazards are found in the project location and their characteristics
        - Sensitivity and exposure (impact) assessment: defines the sensitivities of exposed elements
        - Vulnerability (sensitivity and adaptive capacity) assessment
        - Apply the existing capabilities to get the final level of risk
        - Hazard-exposure-sensitivity ranking and scoring (risk)

5.  **PROPOSED MANAGEMENT AND ADAPTATION ACTIONS**
    *Relate these to the current and existing capabilities. Higher capacities lower the risks.*
    A.  Proposed climate adaptation measures included within the project design.

**Climate Adaptation Plans Within the Project** *(if applicable)*
*Based on the findings of the climate risk assessment discussed in above section 4.0, list all activities being included in the project to address identified significant climate risks.*

| Adaptation Activity | Target Climate Risk |
|---|---|
|  |  |
|  |  |
|  |  |
|  |  |
|  |  |
|  |  |

B.    Possible mitigation measures embedded (or to be embedded) in the project.

**Climate Mitigation Plans within the Project** *(if applicable)*
*Describe project activities and indicators aimed at reducing greenhouse gas emissions.*

| Mitigation Activity | Estimated Greenhouse Gas Emissions Reduction (tons of carbon dioxide equivalent/year) |
|---|---|
| | |
| | |
| | |
| | |
| | |
| | |

C.    Prioritization of identified measures
*For example, cost and benefit analyses, co-benefits, social and political acceptability.*
*The adaptation, as per the National Adaptation Plan of Bangladesh, 2023–2050 (Government of Bangladesh, Ministry of Environment, Forest and Climate Change 2022) and/or mitigation, as per the updated Nationally Determined Contributions 2021 (Government of Bangladesh, Ministry of Environment, Forest and Climate Change 2021) priorities will be selected based on availability of local technology, economic viability, and social acceptability.*

**6.    STAKEHOLDER CONSULTATION AND GROUND VALIDATION**
*Could also involve peer-to-peer interactions, e.g., with engineers who are responsible for the project design and materials. Stakeholders involved are relevant agencies, beneficiaries, and potentially affected communities. If necessary, the draft climate risk screening and climate risk and vulnerability assessment and recommended adaptation options should be justified and verified by visiting project site(s).*

Source: Modified from an Asian Development Bank suggested reporting outline.

# Selected Adaptation Options in Different Ecosystems of Bangladesh

| Ecosystem Type | Vulnerability Contexts Within the Ecosystem | Climate Change Impacts | Key Response Measures[a] |
|---|---|---|---|
| Floodplain ecosystem | • Subject to occasional to regular flooding<br>• Subject to erosion, primarily along major rivers<br>• Subject to moderate to slight drought during Rabi season (mid-October to mid-March)<br>• CFPs are affected by salinity<br>• CFPs are subject to occasional inundation by tidal actions, wave interactions, and cyclonic storm surges | • Increase in extent and duration of floods, high-intensity floods occurring more frequently<br>• High degree of losses and damages (e.g., to crops, infrastructure, homesteads, and manufacturing activities)<br>• Disruption of WASH efforts<br>• Increased spread of disease vectors<br>• Disruption of education<br>• Occasional food insecurity<br>• Increased erosion along erosion-prone rivers<br>• Erosion-induced losses and damages (e.g., infrastructure, dwellings)<br>• Increased drought proneness and crop loss during dry season<br>• Increased salinity ingress along the coastal plains<br>• Salinization<br>• Increased difficulties to find nonsaline surface water in coastal plains<br>• Increased disease burden because of salinity<br>• Increased wave interaction along CFPs (resulting in saline inundation)<br>• Increased risk of drowning in CFPs<br>• Increased loss of livelihoods of coastal fisherfolk | • User-friendly dissemination of early flood warnings<br>• Multipurpose flood shelters<br>• Development and extension of flood-tolerant crop varieties<br>• Enhanced capacity of drainage infrastructure along roads<br>• Greater drainage capacity in urban centers in floodplains<br>• Relocation of manufacturing units from the most vulnerable regions<br>• Improved management of flood control, FCD, and FCDI infrastructure<br>• Improved WASH efforts<br>• Academic infrastructure to be built or rebuilt above record flood danger levels<br>• Geo-engineering-based slope protection of raised plinths (e.g., dwellings, infrastructure)<br>• EWS on riverbank erosion<br>• Relocation of erodible valuable or sensitive infrastructure<br>• Irrigation to address droughts<br>• Improved irrigation/water management<br>• Increased flow volume maintained in rivers or rivulets flowing to the sea<br>• A search for sustainable groundwater tables (instead of exhaustible tiny lenses)<br>• Desalinization of water<br>• Artificially breaking capillary action to safeguard standing crops<br>• Growing crops requiring less water in the dry season, and saline-tolerant crops in CFPs<br>• Enhanced medical support<br>• Refurbishment of weak embankment systems (where social acceptance is high) |

| Ecosystem Type | Vulnerability Contexts Within the Ecosystem | Climate Change Impacts | Key Response Measures[a] |
|---|---|---|---|
| | | | • Design criteria of polders revisited<br>• Innovative EWS for coastal fisherfolks to safeguard livelihoods<br>• Alternative livelihoods promoted (where current livelihoods will not remain useful under climate effects) |
| Barind ecosystem | • Subject to moisture stress at the root zone of preferred crops (i.e., staples)<br>• Lowering of groundwater table during peak dry season, sustained trends of lowering of piezometric surface of groundwater table<br>• Nonavailability of adequate quantum of fresh drinking water because of drying up of hand tube wells | • Adverse health effects because of deterioration of WASH conditions<br>• Much-intensified drought leading to crop loss (primarily boro, but also affecting aman rice potential)<br>• Wheat becoming increasingly nonviable because of high losses incurred<br>• Requirement for irrigation water significantly increases against a reduction in availability of water<br>• Tube wells becoming inoperable during peak dry season<br>• Food insecurity among PEP households, marginalized groups | • Enhanced efforts on WASH<br>• Improved health care services (especially at the grassroots level)<br>• Legal provisioning for boro rice zoning as a function of water availability<br>• Development and dissemination of drought-tolerant crops, crop diversification toward crops requiring less water<br>• Mobilization toward skill enhancement of people dependent on irrigated crops<br>• Excavation or re-excavation of ponds and khals (drainage canals) (where possible) for water retention<br>• Revitalization of SSN programs<br>• Provisioning of knowledge-driven WASH support to PEP and marginalized groups |
| *Haor* ecosystem (Sylhet Basin agroecosystem) | • Subject to *afal* (high-speed gale) and associated high wave interactions<br>• Erosion of raised areas, roadside slopes<br>• Inundation of floodplains resulting in (i) nonavailability of lands for cropping during Kharif-I season (mid-March to mid-July), and (ii) fish breeding and growing opportunities in open water (beneficial) | • Increased flash flood risks that diminish crop (i.e., rice) production potential<br>• Potential loss of food security following early flash floods<br>• Increase in extent and duration of flood (inundation), high-intensity floods occurring more frequently (though the overall effect is small compared to that in other floodplains)<br>• Losses and damages (e.g., to infrastructure, homesteads, manufacturing activities)<br>• *Afal* threatening lives and causing disruption of daily lives<br>• Increased erosion of dwellings and unprotected infrastructure<br>• Disruption of WASH efforts<br>• Increased spread of disease vectors<br>• Disruption of education<br>• Occasional food insecurity<br>• Increased erosion along erosion-prone rivers<br>• Erosion-induced losses and damages (e.g., to infrastructure, dwellings)<br>• Increased drought proneness and crop loss during dry season | • Development and dissemination of flash flood EWS<br>• A shift from paddy to other short-duration crops<br>• Skills enhancement training and market linkage facilitation (value chain) for alternative livelihoods<br>• SSN support (food aid) following occasional crop loss<br>• Increased WASH support and awareness<br>• Slope protection of *haatis* (upland areas), roadside slopes, and other infrastructure (innovative geo-engineering)<br>• Develop robust communication system to offer protection during *afal* (high waves produced by gusty winds)<br>• Improved grassroots-level health care services<br>• Maintenance of submergible embankments (governance aspects)<br>• Vegetative protection of *haatis* (upland areas) and infrastructure (e.g., with *Hijol* (Indian oak) tree, *Koroch* tree, or *binna* (vetiver) grass) |

| Ecosystem Type | Vulnerability Contexts Within the Ecosystem | Climate Change Impacts | Key Response Measures[a] |
|---|---|---|---|
| | | | • Dissemination of knowledge toward enhancing tensile strength of bamboo (i.e., protection material) by means of chemical treatment<br>• Community efforts toward management of *kanda* (rims) of *haatis* (upland areas) |
| *Char* (shallow lands that appear when river water level decreases) ecosystem | • Subject to occasional to regular seasonal inundation or flooding in parts of *chars*<br>• Subject to both erosion and accretion, primarily in *chars* of major rivers, resulting in instability of the *char* lands<br>• Subject to sudden coarse sediment deposition (sand casting), resulting in soil composition that is unsuitable for preferred cultivation<br>• Poor water retention capacity of the topsoil | • Increased severity of bank or edge erosion in the *chars*<br>• Increase in extent and duration of floods<br>• High-intensity floods occurring more frequently<br>• High degree of losses and damages (e.g., to crops, infrastructure, homesteads)<br>• Degradation of WASH infrastructure<br>• Increased spreading of disease vectors<br>• Disruption of education<br>• Occasional food insecurity<br>• Erosion-induced losses and damages (e.g., to infrastructure, dwellings)<br>• Increased moisture stress and crop loss during prolonged dry season<br>• Increased risk of loss of livelihoods because of sand casting | • EWS on riverbank erosion<br>• Relocation of erodible valuable or sensitive infrastructure<br>• User-friendly dissemination of flood EWS<br>• Multipurpose flood shelters for humans and *killas* (raised earthen platform or mounded hill) for livestock relocation during inundation<br>• Development and extension of flood-tolerant and/or short-duration crop varieties<br>• Improved WASH efforts, with design components in the infrastructure that are detachable and re-installable as necessary<br>• Academic infrastructure to be built or rebuilt above record flood danger levels<br>• Geo-engineering-based slope protection of raised plinths (e.g., dwellings, infrastructure)<br>• Pit cultivation system to optimize water use in sandy soils<br>• Irrigation to fight moisture stress<br>• Improved irrigation or water management (optimizing irrigation water demand, water conservation, water retention, and water efficiency)<br>• Livelihoods diversification to facilitate out-migration in urban centers<br>• Academic calendar adjustment according to annual water cycle<br>• Administrative, academic, and rural market infrastructure built on stilts |
| Coastal ecosystem | • CFPs are affected by salinity (which is primarily because of conditions created by the operation of Farakka Dam) | • Occasional floods and waterlogging have much-pronounced coverage<br>• High degree of losses and damages (e.g., crops, infrastructure, homesteads, manufacturing activities)<br>• Nonavailability of nonsaline drinking water | • Continued efforts of cyclone preparedness program<br>• Increased flow regime to be maintained in the sea-going coastal rivers<br>• Multipurpose cyclone shelters (in accordance with population density) |

| Ecosystem Type | Vulnerability Contexts Within the Ecosystem | Climate Change Impacts | Key Response Measures[a] |
|---|---|---|---|
| | • Coastal river systems are affected by seasonal distribution of flow; CFPs are subject to occasional inundation by tidal actions, wave interactions, and cyclonic storm surges<br>• The northward movement of a freshwater-saline mixing zone in coastal rivers along with siltation of riverbeds give rise to waterlogging in certain locations in the southwest and south-central regions<br>• Coastal erosion has been shrinking a few highly populated islands, threatening other islands | • Disruption of WASH efforts<br>• Increased difficulties to find nonsaline surface water in coastal plains<br>• Increased spreading of disease vectors<br>• Disruption of education<br>• Crop loss and food insecurity in smallholder households<br>• Increased erosion along erosion-prone rivers and sea-facing islands<br>• Erosion-induced losses and damages (e.g., infrastructure, dwellings)<br>• Increased salinity ingress along the coastal plains, salinization<br>• Increased disease burden because of salinity<br>• Increased wave interaction along sea-facing unprotected lands (resulting in saline inundation)<br>• Increased loss of livelihoods and assets (e.g., fishing boats) of coastal fisherfolk | • Development and extension of saline tolerant crop varieties (rice and non-rice)<br>• Enhanced capacity of drainage infrastructure along polders<br>• Greater drainage capacity in urban centers in coastal plains<br>• Relocation of manufacturing units from the most vulnerable regions<br>• Improved management of water infrastructure (e.g., sluice operation, embankment management)<br>• Improved WASH efforts<br>• Academic infrastructure to be built or rebuilt above record surge danger levels (leaving adequate draft height underneath)<br>• Relocation of erodible valuable or sensitive infrastructure<br>• A search for sustainable groundwater tables (instead of exhaustible tiny lenses), desalinization of water<br>• Artificially breaking capillary action to safeguard standing crops<br>• Selection and promotion of saline-tolerant crops in CFPs<br>• Enhanced medical care support<br>• Refurbishment of weak embankment systems (where social acceptance is high)<br>• Resuscitation of choked *khals* (drainage canals) and rivulets to improve drainage<br>• Design criteria of polders revisited<br>• Innovative EWS for coastal fisherfolks to safeguard livelihoods<br>• Alternative livelihoods promoted (where current livelihoods will not remain useful under climate effects)<br>• Skills enhancement training supported and value chain facilitated toward diversifying livelihoods<br>• Safe out-migration facilitated through policies, skills enhancement, and advocacy |

CFP = coastal floodplain; EWS = early warning system; FCD = flood control and drainage; FCDI = flood control, drainage, and irrigation; PEP = poor and extremely poor; SSN = social safety net; WASH = water, sanitation, and hygiene.

[a]  Key response measures to be included in the project design will depend on factors such as specific project location, sector and subsector coverage, and objectives. As such, the adaptation measures will vary within a given ecosystem, because of differences in project design and cost.

Source: Government of Bangladesh, Ministry of Planning, Planning Commission, General Economics Division. 2014. *Development Project Proforma/Proposal Manual (Instructions for Preparing Development Project Proposal)—Parts 1 and 2: Appendixes.* Dhaka.

# Glossary

| | | |
|---|---|---|
| **adaptation** | — | an adjustment process to the actual or expected climate and its effects. In human systems, adaptation seeks to moderate harm or exploit beneficial opportunities. In natural systems, human intervention may facilitate adjustment to the expected climate and its effects (United Nations International Strategy for Disaster Reduction 2009). |
| **exposure** | — | the situation of people, infrastructure, housing, production capacities, and other tangible human assets located in hazard-prone areas. Measures of exposure can include the number of people or types of assets in an area. These can be combined with the specific vulnerability and capacity of the exposed elements to any particular hazard to estimate the quantitative risks associated with that hazard in the area of interest (United Nations International Strategy for Disaster Reduction 2009). |
| **hazard** | — | a process, phenomenon, or human activity that may cause loss of life, injury, or other health impacts, property damage, social and economic disruption, or environmental degradation. Hazards may be natural, anthropogenic, or socio-natural in origin. Natural hazards are predominantly associated with natural processes and phenomena. Anthropogenic hazards are induced entirely or predominantly by human activities and choices. This term does not include the occurrence or risk of armed conflicts and other situations of social instability or tension that are subject to international humanitarian law and national legislation. Several hazards are socio-natural, in that they are associated with a combination of natural and anthropogenic factors, including environmental degradation and climate change (United Nations International Strategy for Disaster Reduction 2009). |
| **impacts** | — | the total effect, including negative effects (e.g., economic losses) and positive effects (e.g., economic gains), of a hazardous event or a disaster. The term includes economic, human, and environmental impacts, and may include death, injuries, diseases, and other negative effects on human physical, mental, and social well-being (United Nations International Strategy for Disaster Reduction 2009). |
| **mitigation** | — | reduction of greenhouse gas emissions that contribute to global warming and climate change (United Nations International Strategy for Disaster Reduction 2009). |

**resilience** — the ability of a system, community, or society exposed to hazards to resist, absorb, accommodate, adapt to, transform, and recover from the effects of a hazard in a timely and efficient manner, including through the preservation and restoration of its essential basic structures and functions through risk management (United Nations International Strategy for Disaster Reduction 2009).

**risk** — the potential loss of life, injury, or destroyed or damaged assets that could occur to a system, society, or a community in a specific period, determined probabilistically as a function of hazard, exposure, vulnerability, and capacity. The definition of disaster risk reflects the concept of hazardous events and disasters as the outcome of continuously present conditions of risk. Disaster risk comprises different types of potential losses, which are often difficult to quantify (United Nations International Strategy for Disaster Reduction 2009).

**vulnerability** — the conditions determined by physical, social, economic, and environmental factors or processes that increase the susceptibility of an individual, a community, assets, or systems to the impacts of hazards (United Nations International Strategy for Disaster Reduction 2009).

ary

# References

Abedin, J. et al. 2020. An Investigation of the Characteristics, Causes, and Consequences of June 13, 2017 Landslides in Rangamati District, Bangladesh. *Geoenvironmental Disasters*. 7 (23).

Abedin, J. and H. Khatun. 2020. Impacts of Flash Flood on Livelihood and Adaptation Strategies of the *Haor* Inhabitants: A Study in Tanguar *Haor* of Sunamganj, Bangladesh. *The Dhaka University Journal of Earth and Environmental Sciences* 8 (1). pp. 41–51.

Ahmad, H. 2019. Bangladesh Coastal Zone Management Status and Future Trends. *Journal of Coastal Zone Management*. 22 (1).

Ali, A. 1996. Vulnerability of Bangladesh to Climate Change and Sea Level Rise through Tropical Cyclones and Storm Surges. *Water, Air, and Soil Pollution*. 92. pp. 171–179.

Anas, A. Z. M. 2019. Bangladesh's Disappearing River Lands. *The New Humanitarian*. 29 August. https://www.thenewhumanitarian.org/Bangladesh-river-erosion-engulfs-homes-climate -change-migration.

Asia Foundation. 2012. *A Situation Analysis of Climate Change Adaptation Initiatives in Bangladesh*. Dhaka. https://innovation.brac.net/fif2016/images/library/SituationAnalysisofCCinitiatives.pdf.

Asian Development Bank (ADB). 2014. *Climate Risk Management in ADB Projects*. Manila. https://www.adb.org/ sites/default/files/publication/148796/climate-risk-management-adb-projects.pdf.

ADB. 2015. *Bangladesh: Capacity Building for Disaster Risk Finance*. Consultant's report. Manila (TA 8144-BAN).

ADB. 2016. *Guidelines for Climate Proofing Investment in the Water Sector: Water Supply and Sanitation*. Manila. https://www.adb.org/sites/default/files/institutional-document/219646/guidelines-climate-proofing -water.pdf.

Asikunnaby et al. 2021. *Multi-Hazard Risk Analysis of Climate-Related Disasters in Bangladesh*. London: Start Fund Bangladesh; Start Network; and Network for Information, Response and Preparedness Activities on Disaster. https://bangladesh.un.org/sites/default/files/2022-01/Multi-Hazard%20Risk%20Analysis%20 in%20Bangladesh_Final%20Report.pdf.

Dasgupta, S. et al. 2014. Cyclones in a Changing Climate: The Case of Bangladesh. *Climate and Development*. 6 (2). https://www.tandfonline.com/doi/abs/10.1080/17565529.2013.868335.

Eckstein, D., V. Künzel, and L. Schäfer. 2021. *Global Climate Risk Index 2021: Who Suffers Most from Extreme Weather Events? Weather-Related Loss Events in 2019 and 2000–2019*. Bonn: Germanwatch. https://www.germanwatch.org/sites/default/files/Global%20Climate%20Risk%20Index%202021_2.pdf.

Germanwatch. 2004. *Sea Level Rise in Bangladesh and the Netherlands. One Phenomenon, Many Consequences*. https://germanwatch.org/sites/default/files/publication/3642.pdf.

Government of Bangladesh, Geological Survey of Bangladesh. 2000. *Earthquake Zone Map*. Dhaka.

Government of Bangladesh, Ministry of Agriculture, Bangladesh Agricultural Research Council. 2000. *Pre-Kharif Drought Prone Areas Map*. Dhaka.

Government of Bangladesh, Ministry of Disaster Management and Relief. 2019. *Standing Orders on Disaster 2019*. Dhaka.

Government of Bangladesh, Ministry of Environment and Forests. 2009. *Bangladesh Climate Change Strategy and Action Plan 2009*. Dhaka. http://nda.erd.gov.bd/files/1/Publications/CC%20Policy%20Documents/ BCCSAP2009.pdf.

Government of Bangladesh; Ministry of Environment, Forest and Climate Change. 2021. *Nationally Determined Contributions 2021 (updated)*. Dhaka. https://unfccc.int/sites/default/files/NDC/2022-06/NDC _submission_20210826revised.pdf.

Government of Bangladesh; Ministry of Environment, Forest and Climate Change. 2022. *National Adaptation Plan of Bangladesh 2023–2050*. Dhaka. https://www4.unfccc.int/sites/SubmissionsStaging/Documents/ 202211020942---National%20Adaptation%20Plan%20of%20Bangladesh%20(2023-2050).pdf.

Government of Bangladesh, Ministry of Housing and Public Works, Housing and Building Research Institute. 2017. *Bangladesh National Building Code*. http://www.hbri.gov.bd/site/page/a5c13d7e-212d-4a16-bbf9- 3e1ad937ba56/বাংলাদেশ-জাতীয়-বিল্ডিং-কোড-(BNBC).

Government of Bangladesh, Ministry of Planning, Planning Commission and ADB. 2021. *Bangladesh Climate and Disaster Risk Atlas*. Dhaka and Manila. Two Volumes – https://www.adb.org/publications/bangladesh- climate-disaster-risk-atlas-volume-1 and https://www.adb.org/publications/bangladesh-climate-disaster- risk-atlas-volume-2.

Government of Bangladesh, Ministry of Planning, Planning Commission, General Economics Division (GED). 2014. *Development Project Proforma/Proposal Manual (Instructions for Preparing Development Project Proposal)—Parts 1 and 2: Appendixes*. Dhaka.

Government of Bangladesh, Ministry of Planning, Planning Commission, GED. 2018. *Bangladesh Delta Plan 2100: Bangladesh in the 21st Century—The Best Gift for the Future Generations by the Present Generation*. Dhaka. https://oldweb.lged.gov.bd/UploadedDocument/UnitPublication/1/756/BDP%202100%20Abridged%20 Version%20English.pdf.

Government of Bangladesh, Ministry of Planning, Planning Commission, GED. 2020. *Eighth Five Year Plan (July 2020–June 2025): Promoting Prosperity and Fostering Inclusiveness.* Dhaka. https://plancomm.gov.bd/sites/default/files/files/plancomm.portal.gov.bd/files/68e32f08_13b8_4192_ab9b_abd5a0a62a33/2021-02-03-17-04-ec95e78e452a813808a483b3b22e14a1.pdf.

Government of Bangladesh, Ministry of Planning, Planning Commission, Planning Division. 2022. *Guidelines for Formulation, Appraisal, Approval and Revision of Development Projects in the Public Sector.* Dhaka.

Haque, S. A. 2006. Salinity Problems and Crop Production in Coastal Regions of Bangladesh. *Pakistan Journal of Botany.* 38 (5). pp. 1359–1365.

Hasnat, M. A. 2018. Over 160,000 Hectares Lost to Padma, Jamuna in Four Decades. *Dhaka Tribune.* 12 October. https://www.dhakatribune.com/bangladesh/nation/2018/10/12/over-160-000-hectares-lost-to-padma-jamuna-in-four-decades.

Hussain, A. 2017. Cyclone Fatalities Fall, Economic Losses on Rise. *Dhaka Tribune.* 30 April. https://www.dhakatribune.com/bangladesh/2017/04/30/cyclone-fatalities-fall-economic-losses-rise.

Inman, M. 2009. Where Warming Hits Hard. *Nature Climate Change.* 3. pp. 18–21. https://www.nature.com/articles/climate.2009.3.

Islam, T. and R. E. Peterson. 2009. Climatology of Landfalling Tropical Cyclones in Bangladesh 1877–2003. *Natural Hazards.* 48. pp. 115–135.

Japan International Cooperation Agency (JICA). 2019a. *JICA Climate-FIT (Adaptation): Climate Finance Impact Tool for Adaptation, Guidance on Climate Risk Assessment and Adaptation.* Tokyo. https://www.jica.go.jp/activities/issues/climate/ku57pq00001o9h2v-att/climate_fit_e.pdf.

JICA. 2019b. *JICA Climate-FIT (Mitigation): Climate Finance Impact Tool for Mitigation, Quantitative Evaluation of GHG Emissions Reduction (Removals).* Tokyo. https://www.jica.go.jp/english/our_work/thematic_issues/climate/fh2q4d000000phkh-att/guidline.pdf.

Khalil, G. M. 1992. Cyclones and Storm Surges in Bangladesh: Some Mitigative Measures. *Natural Hazards.* 6. pp. 11–24.

Needs Assessment Working Group. 2022. *Gap Analysis: North East Flash Flood Response 2022, Bangladesh.* https://www.humanitarianresponse.info/sites/www.humanitarianresponse.info/files/documents/files/20221207_nawg_gap_analysis_ne_flood_2022_final.pdf.

Notre Dame Global Adaptation Initiative. 2021. *Country Profile: Bangladesh.* https://gain.nd.edu/assets/254505/nd_gain_bangladesh_analysis.pdf.

Ozaki, M. 2016. Disaster Risk Financing in Bangladesh. *ADB South Asia Working Paper Series.* No. 46. Manila: ADB. https://www.adb.org/sites/default/files/publication/198561/sawp-046.pdf.

ReliefWeb. 2017. *Bangladesh: Floods and Landslides*. 1 September. https://reliefweb.int/disaster/ls-2017-000068-bgd.

Roy, P. 2014. New Hope for Erosion-Hit Bangladesh. *The Third Pole*. 18 September.  https://www.thethirdpole.net/2014/09/18/new-hope-for-erosion-hit-bangladesh.

Sarwar, M. G. M. 2005. *Impacts of Sea Level Rise on the Coastal Zone of Bangladesh*. Lund, Sweden: Lund University International Masters Programme in Environmental Science. https://www.lumes.lu.se/sites/lumes.lu.se/files/golam_sarwar.pdf.

Sarwar, M. G. M. 2008. *Landslide Tragedy of Bangladesh*. Paper prepared for the first World Landslide Forum. 18–21 November 2008. Tokyo.

Sarwar, M. G. M. 2013. Sea Level Rise Along the Coast of Bangladesh. In R. Shaw, F. Mallick, and A. Islam, eds. *Disaster Risk Reduction Approaches in Bangladesh*. New York: Springer.

Sarwar, M. G. M., S. Nabi, and M. Shafin. 2016. *Loss and Damage Perspective of Tropical Storm Roanu*. Dhaka: Christian Aid Bangladesh. https://www.academia.edu/36657774/Loss_and_Damage_Roanu_Bangladesh_Coast_pdf.

Sarwar, M. G. M. and C. Woodroffe. 2013. Rates of Shoreline Change Along the Coast of Bangladesh. *Journal of Coastal Conservation*. 17 (3). pp. 515–526.

United Nations International Strategy for Disaster Reduction. 2009. *2009 Terminology on Disaster Risk Reduction*. https://www.unisdr.org/files/7817_UNISDRTerminologyEnglish.pdf.

United States Agency for International Development. 2018. *Climate Risk Profile: Bangladesh*. https://www.climatelinks.org/sites/default/files/asset/document/2018-02-Mar_CadmusCISF_Climate-Risk-Profile-Bangladesh.pdf.

World Bank. 2000. *Bangladesh: Climate Change and Sustainable Development*. Report No. 21104-BD. Dhaka. https://documents1.worldbank.org/curated/en/906951468743377163/pdf/multi0page.pdf.

World Bank. 2010. *Economics of Adaptation to Climate Change: Bangladesh*. Washington, DC. https://openknowledge.worldbank.org/server/api/core/bitstreams/bbf540c6-b18f-55b5-96ce-e49dc7e3e605/content.

WorldData.Info. 2023. *Cyclones in Bangladesh*. https://www.worlddata.info/asia/bangladesh/cyclones.php.